MEG REYNOLDS

INLANDIA INSTITUTE
RIVERSIDE, CALIFORNIA

Meg Reynolds

PRAISE FOR *CONDITION*

We are born with "so little language," Meg Reynolds writes in *Condition*. Yet in these poems, there is so much of it, visual and textual, articulating maternal devotion... Rigorous poetic technique, equilibrium and confidence in each textual and visual composition draw us nearer to the answer to the question: how close can we ever get to what we make, be it art, or a child?
—OCTAVIO QUINTANILLA

Meg Reynolds' *Condition* is a beautiful and unflinching vision of mothering, morphing, and being, couched in the bodily lyricism of life. *Condition* [is] an astounding story of motherhood in which the mythic and the momentary continually collide.
—MARK LEIDNER

In *Condition*, [Meg Reynolds] illuminates a postpartum world during quarantine, revealing a speaker "ravenous and bewildered," her exhaustion mixed with "animal joy." Here, domesticity is always laced with the feral, woven with folklore and oracles, the beauty and terror of the ancient woods. *Condition* is incandescent, lit with primal love and rage, braided with imagination and grit.
—DIANA WHITNEY

In Meg Reynolds' visceral alchemy, we recover & recover only to be rent open & made to bear again. This *Condition*—of rage, fear, sickness, insomnia—coupled with joy, coupled with love—blooms strange familiar magic thanks to a craft that shines like a bruise.

—Jennifer Sperry Steinorth

In confinement, and in the intense physical closeness of new motherhood, the body blurs into fable and allegory, our most primal alphabet. These immersive poems take the reader into both dreamstate and absolute clarity of vision.

—Rachel Richardson

For Nana
& my mother
& all those who
look after anyone

Condition by Meg Reynolds

ISBN: 978-1-955969-52-9
Library of Congress Control Number: 2026932242

Permissions
Inlandia Institute
4178 Chestnut Street
Riverside, CA 92501

Executive Director: Cati Porter
Book Layout & Design: Kenji C. Liu
Cover Artist: Meg Reynolds

Printed and bound in the United States
Distributed by Ingram

Published by Inlandia Institute
Riverside, California
www.InlandiaInstitute.org
First Edition

Table of Contents

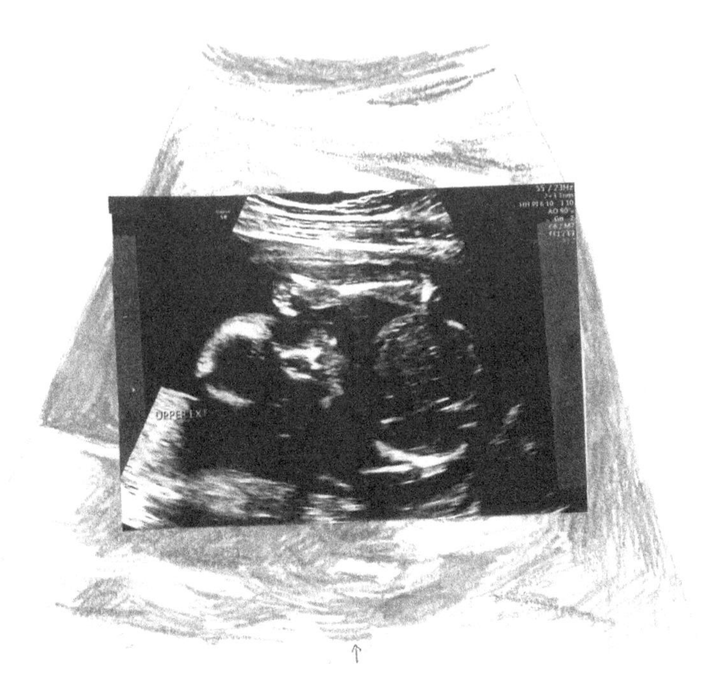

Folktale

You were once a daughter to a comfortable nothingness.
You looked down on the whole earth, searched
and searched until the glint of your near eyes, supple
and primordial as a hagfish's, fell on a rocky hill
   in November.

There was a woman in the far below, a blot of navy and
denim in the burnished tangle of stick season.
She followed two men and a boy up a rocky hill in a brace
of ice rain. The herd moved up and around
   them—Holsteins,
big and fitful, spooked on the incline, hooves shining
like dimes in the cold. They walked, sidestepping stones
and erratic hooves, to move the animals to an
   upper pasture.

When they came back to the ochre light of the barn,
a calf head was emerging from the back end of her mother.
You watched as the farmer tied a length of teal twine
to each of the calf's protruding white hooves. The hooves
crossed daintily under the calf's chin, the calf whose head
nodded at the efforts of her own expulsion. The farmer
handed one length of twine to the woman. Together
they pulled and the cow lowed and the calf slipped free
before slapping onto the stone floor at their feet.

The woman looked down and said, *Welcome to the world*,
and dragged the calf into the hay under her mother's

warm mouth. It was then that you made your decision. At the bare thrill on the woman's face, a flash you witnessed,

the woman became a door.

Song

Down with the tremulous head voice.

Relinquish the yellow ballooning cries.

Stretch the scale down to the thud of an

elephant heart. In the gut, there's

a gong you can hammer a mallet on.

The mouth and the jaw and the pelvis let

go. May you deepen like throat singers

echoing water. Sing lower. Your

hips are a chariot plummeting

thousands of octaves. Opening,

opening, maw in the blackness through

which you will pass a singular

scorched and seething star.

Labor

All my loyal exiles came back:

The cloying one who shows
her underbelly in a bid for love

the drunk,
the stripped,
the beggar, the flirt

the chorus of alligators
and bovine and scavengers,
the contender, lean and famished

the little girl who twists a quilt
in her fists was the one to let
her small voice out between the teeth
and ask for an epidural

They threaded the needle
into the defeated king
who bore down and denied the voltaic
slip of pain. And then

it was the nobody, the zero, who scratched
red tracks across the belly,
went weak and puddling,
who nurses rotated hourly

My perfection, a long mirage,
was of no help
My gilded valor failed to arrive

My daughter had to pass through the swarm
   of multitudes,
the worst of her mother made into gates,
to shoulder herself out

They all came though they knew
how they clot my craw with hate, knew
I would send them back
to their hovels of bone

To let them stay
would mean finding
a place for all of us here

Bath

The nurse takes her under the spout
and scrubs away the vernix, her waxy shroud,
with a smear of gold soap. Bells of water

ring off the sink. My heart lifts and clinks
down like an exhaust flapper. Under my alloyed
throat a primal mechanism spins inside,

and I steam with awe. Here, in the basement
of the hospital, the nurse flips the baby
under the stream like she's handling a fish.

I have been asked to remember many
very old miracles, lines devoted to war
and the endless paths to the abyss.

And I did, ravenous and bewildered.
There is no other way to describe what I feel now.
A descent has begun in this bright room.

9 Months in Quarantine

Absence of my mother in the delivery room

of my mother, my aunt, my grandmother
when I failed at breastfeeding
and my daughter sheered down
to red and brittle

of my friends as I sweat and cried
over the incandescence
of the child on my chest

when her father returned to work
when her fever spiked
when she threw up in her crib
when she was too weak to cry

The aloneness of it:
wind whistling through a skull

Milkstone

AFTER WOLFGANG LAIB

We taped a tube as slender as a dandelion stem
to my finger and I guided both
into my daughter's mouth. The tube
rested at the corner of her lips. The soft pad
of my pinky pressed at her palate,
and she nursed fruitlessly. Then her father
pushed down the stopper on the syringe
filled with 10 mL of breastmilk,
slow and then slower. It spread into her,
softening her limbs. She was
a thin place, fragile as wet paper.
I remembered the artist who slowly poured
milk onto a beveled slab of white marble
up to the absolute rim without spilling.
The edges of the stone disappeared and left
a square of white like a window into
a lit infinite. There was an anguish
to her smallness and a gore to giving
birth to your own heart. She drank
the last milliliter and slept.

IS MAKING MINERVA LIKE MAKING A POEM?
IF SO, DID I BECOME HER DEAD AUTHOR WHEN SHE
CAME OUT (OF ME)?
FOR HER TO BE (HERSELF, ANYTHING) DOES SHE REQUIRE
A GREATER & GREATER DISTANCE FROM THE STARTING POINT
OF MY UTERUS?
IS SHE THE LONE ARBITER OF HER PARTICULARITY,
TO BE READ & GUESSED AT EVERYWHERE (BY ME, ESPECIALLY)?
OR IS SHE A STUDENT OF OLDER LITERARY TRADITIONS?
A DISTILLATION OF OUR ANCESTRY, ENDOWING ME,
HER MAKER, WITH PROFOUND AUTHORIAL POWER?
OR ARE WE BOTH ALIVE, READING EACH OTHER?
IS SHE, WITH HER RECKLESSLY BEAUTIFUL, LONG FINGERS
THAT ONCE FLUTTERED LIKE MOTHS IN THE LOW OF ME,
THE SUBJECT I CONTINUALLY DISAPPEAR INTO?
WHAT IS A MOTHER? A PLACE, A NAME,
THE SITE FROM WHICH SHE TRANSGRESSES?
(A, THE, MY) CHILD, FROM OR THROUGH?

Bad latch

Two days in and ounces fall from your frame.
You can't afford to lose more. The neighborhood
around the house looks dim and abandoned.

I blame myself for your hunger. While you sleep,
the stun of dread really builds momentum,
becomes what fills the absence of sleep.

There was the night I showed up wine drunk,
missing a rain boot, at an ex's house ready
to give myself to him like a flood-soaked dog.

I want to confess it to you, what you're getting.
You look so much like me as I was then: your bald
and befuddled need. This is just one of the replays,

the familiar units of shame I review to give
my new shame company. Everything I have
and have ever been rushes forward

to face you, skinny child,
and begs you to slant
away from ruin.

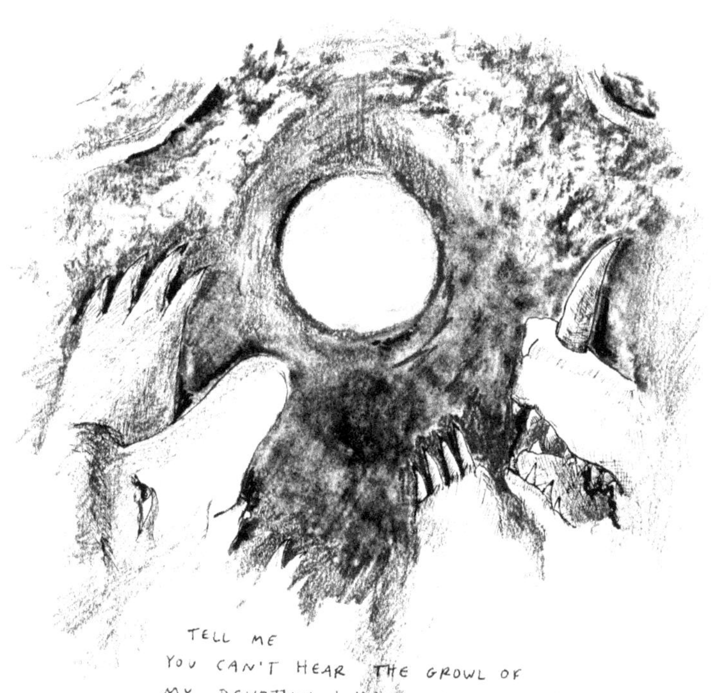

TELL ME
YOU CAN'T HEAR THE GROWL OF
MY DEVOTION. I HAVE LANGUAGE IN MY
THROAT I HAVE BEEN SAVING
FOR THE PURPOSE.

11 Months in Quarantine

Many are thrilled to open
the back door and let this year out.
The year that came to us like
an intruder and showed us we are not

the heroes we'd hoped to be. We'd lie
in our beds happy if it would just
leave quietly with what it's stolen.
This is the year we married

and conceived our daughter.
She arrived and forced hope on us.
She fills the house with cries.
I open my dress and wait

for the let down, glittered
with sting, listen for the click
in her throat. Whatever comes,
there is no unringing the bell of her.

Hungry

When she wants
to eat, she places her palm

on my cheek and turns
my head until

my chin rests in her mouth.
She nurses there

like foal at a stone
of salt. What she does

with so little language:
takes the softest vowels,

smoothed free of
the clatter of consonants,

those blunt interruptions
of her longing,

and makes
her demands.

Witching Hour

The secret is
it is all invented:
the systems, schedules,
the grand expectations
are tensile, fibrous, arbitrary.
This becomes obvious
between midnight and 4 AM
where night is spongy and yielding.
Here I am, eyes ablaze
as roman candles,
hair flat to my head,
so it appears absent
in this place where the darkness
disappears plenty,
the rhythm of my breath
unrecognizable
as I lean over my child
with a hanging breast.
I am not everything,
but a milked
and electric anything.

THREE MONTHS
POSTPARTUM, MY
BIRTH-SOFTENED
BODY

13 Months in Quarantine

We push furniture back and forth
across the nursery for long months inside.
I hang a print of Edward Hopper's
House by the Railroad

over the changing table.
Hopper is known as a renderer
of isolation, but he insisted
he painted only the facts.

This from a man who isolated
with his wife, Jo, voluntarily, violently,
virtuosically for decades, both dying
in the same apartment in the same year.

Now the baby's here and stares at the house
while I change her diaper. Her gaze crosses
and recrosses the train tracks that lead
to an elsewhere she never sees. We stay

inside. It's safer here where I press
and milk jets across the couch before
I thread her mouth to my breast
with a thin line so white it is blue.

Idleness

When she sleeps in my arms, I am alone in the quiet,
motionless as I've ever been. Neighbors pass under
the window. One says to the other, *Ever hear the one
about the farmer who hired a demon to work his farm?*

I have. When the farmer signed the contract
with his tired blood, the devil warned him, *He will
find a task for himself if you don't*. And yet,
in mere weeks, forgetfulness overcomes him
and the farmer neglects to set the demon to his tasks.
When the farmer gets home, he finds a fire pit
in the middle of the kitchen floor and, above it
on the roasting spit, is the neighbor's child.

What a terrible story and that I should tell it now
while my own child sleeps in my arms. The burn
of my brain crackles above her. Who is it
that turns on the spit? And who, oh hell,
is turning it?

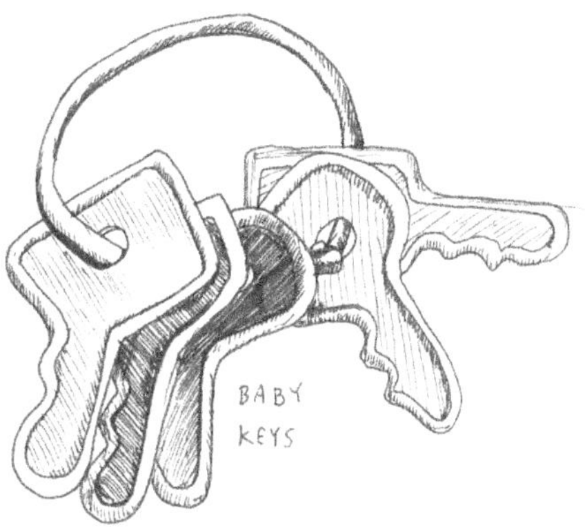
BABY
KEYS

15 Months in Quarantine

The walls of the house stand fast
against the snow. From the poured concrete
foundation to the shingles, the clack of siding,
it does its steady job. How strange

that snow is soft but could bury you.
Minnie gums two fingers
on her right hand and watches
from my lap. I have always wanted

a daughter and a window, nothing to do
but watch flakes cut through the cold air
outside. What a deep winter,
sickness haunting the space

between everyone like static.
We can't go anywhere today just
like the other days. Here
we find a set of constraints:

a few characters, a single setting,
the rise of tension toward
an unpredictable breaking point.
I am afraid of the fact that

tragic endings can satisfy a distant
audience. I look around and find
the makings of a small family
drama or a horror film or a joke.

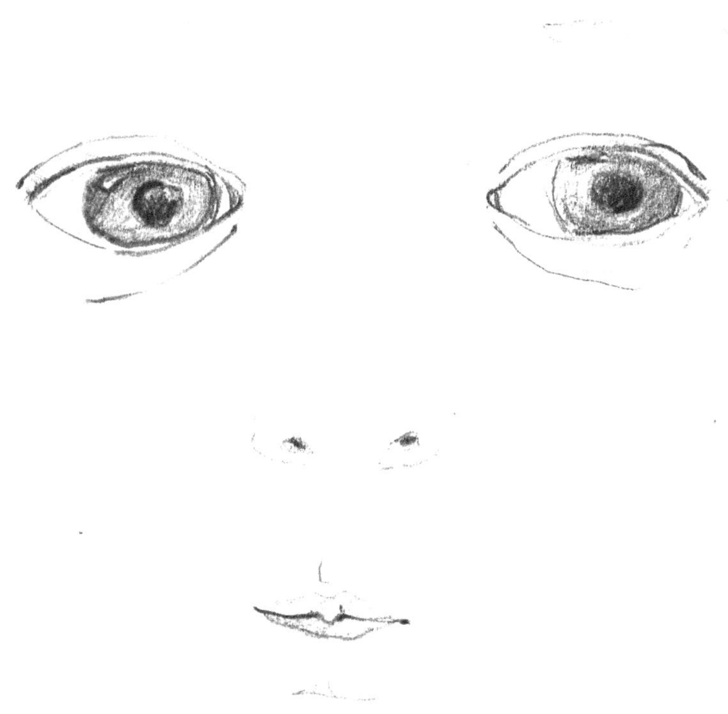

Plums

At birth, my daughter's mouth
was so small that her latch raised blisters
on my nipples as black as plums.

The nurse put her face close to mine,
See that? Get her to open her mouth!
In the teaspoon cellar of my heart, a place

as damp as fruit stones, I nursed my anger
to full ripening. To ask my baby to open
her mouth any farther would

have been pulling her apart. How
to explain to a stranger that my daughter
will be the monarch of her own jaw?

She deigns to unfold. She demands
and harangues. Even her petulance
seems ordained. I serve her hungers

with an obsequious joy. She wants and I give
nourishment bright as camphor.
I kneel on the carpet with my offerings:

plum and cardamom jam in yogurt,
a sliver of strawberry. She shivers
against it, the cells of her a cloud

of sheep herded to pasture, to pleasure,
her body finding home in it
from the broken plate of my hands.

Tire Change

You come home from work, and I tuck my fingers
in your waistband. You made an appointment
for me at Costco. New tires.
I've been alone with the baby all day,
and this is where you've sent me. The fluorescent aisles
are the opposite of the space between your neck
and shoulder where your smell hums.
It's already dark outside when I get here.

The servicemen lit in their big garage boxes
look out from under the cars and call to me
from the weak shadows. I sit in a folding chair
beneath a row of tires, the hot stink of rubber
coming down in sheets, and scroll
my phone like a teenager.

Half the night is wasted. I have wasted
half my life wanting to be elsewhere.
I married a man who leaves it to me
to panic with longing.

Isn't this just a big tease? It's your sexy game
to assign these responsible, domestic tasks,
to send me out so I can come back.
You know what I'm like. That I would sit here
hating you for being so helpful
and half-dressed on the other side of town.

FROM BENEATH THE OVERPASS
I WATCH AS SMOKE RISES
THROUGH THE EVERGREENS
IN A WAVERING WHITE COLUMN.
IT TURNS IN THE WIND
WITH THE THREADY CERTAINTY
OF AN APPROACHING ANIMAL,
A SUPPLE JOINT. THIS IS HOW
THOUGHTS COME NOW
AS AN UNGULATE AT THE BANK
OF THE RIVER, WATCHFUL,
WAITING TO SEE IF I
WILL RISE OR HOW DANGEROUS
I WILL PROVE TO BE.

Collision

The winter sky is crumpled laundry: sheets
of ashen sleet and dish rags, diaper

decay and slush. A woman in a sedan
slides across the traffic like

she's rushing into my embrace. When control
loses grip of you—snapping

free by a few gray hairs—and you float away
in an open jacket, you become

nameless as Grendel's mother, ripe as fur
in cavelight, a shuffling mosaic

of lived-in denim, flesh, and hair ties thrown
on asphalt. For a moment you

are weightless, free again. The chaos loves
you, asks for nothing. It is easy

to slide into monstrosity, to take
a certain pleasure in letting yourself

go wild on no sleep, hunger and stink, driving
home, newly sculpted with violence.

Scholars refer to Grendel's mother

with names like *hagbride, bitchmother,*

derived from old translations of Valkyrie.
I let the other driver hit

me, let her put me in my place. My name
is on my insurance cards. But when I

get home my daughter is crying in blares like a war horn.
The volume mauls my brain. I rise

and sniff her out, snuff out her wants, our thirsts
entwined in animal joy. Colliding

like atoms, we divulge our natures here,
scattered tightly in the dark.

17 Months in Quarantine

After we nurse, my daughter lifts her head, the size
and weight of a pearled nautilus, and practices
her human sounds. Her speech is akin to song,
her eyes wide with a shock of satisfied lucidity.

The future in her, she quakes as though she is
still arriving in ecstatic layers. It could, however,
be me that vibrates like the yellows
of *No. 14/No. 10 (Yellow Greens)*: amber, saffron,

tawny, blond, all the shades in the sunstruck window
to the left of the couch. Many look at Rothko's paintings
and think, *My kid could do that*. Sure they could,
but not with paint. There's no canvas aching

around the stretchers. It's a baby, a fresh
person, an aural expanse, sand and xanthous,
a door through which I've stepped, never to return.
Isn't that what any artist wants, for someone

to stand before what you've made
and feel the cogs and springs within them
flashing into action, an alteration cell by cell?
I flare over her as she sleeps. I am so close.

SHE DOES NOT HEAR
THE HOURS AS
THEY WHINE PAST US,
DOESN'T REALIZE
HOW I'VE FAILED
TO SLOW TIME.

Nothing

I wonder if I do enough. I wait, feed you, let the weather of your vernal moods move in and out of the apartment like the weather that followed your making where I did nothing and you fattened and fell from me. In the long somnolent days of your infancy, where you slept by your own internal timepiece, I did nothing, no sleep. I just lay beside you in the warm glow of your surviving the night or walked and walked the neighborhood to find the record of the wind left in the long grass. We are in the rooms of our foremothers. In the evening, relief was a vast contemplative darkness hung around the fire. The larger forces of the world moved through and toward them like animals crossing the forest to their own rest.

SHE HAS A STILLNESS & SYMMETRY LIKE THE GOLDEN MASK OF AGAMEMNON SHIMMERING ON THE EDGE OF LIVING. AS SERENE IN SLEEP AS KEATS IN PLASTER, NAPOLEON IN MARBLE, MAHLER IN WAX, SHE IS DELICATE & SWEET AS THOUGH HER FACE IS RENDERED IN SUGAR. I AM ONLY CERTAIN OF AMBIGUITY: SHE IS MORE THAN A CRUST OF SNOW, GOLD BENT OVER WOOD BUT COULDN'T SHE COLLAPSE AGAINST A BREATH TO REVEAL A VOID INTO WHICH I WOULD FALL FOREVER? LOOKING & LOOKING DOWN, SHOW ME THE EVIDENCE OF HER POWER. NOT THESE PETALS OF DEAD MEN. USELESSLY, THE FIST OF MY HEART DEMANDS SHE DENY THAT PART OF HERSELF.

Deprivation

The air hisses and greens.   The cabinets are open.
Bars   of moonlight cast   through ice at the
  roofline
and carve the shape of her   face as she floats
between states of waking   and rest. The light
is so cool,   here, in   the specter of what is
lost. I walk knocked   lopsided, a knot
of matted hair   on my head. What
does my child think of me?   Black flags snap
in my peripheral vision.   My face, a pale beacon.
Electricity coughs   from the outlets.
The knives   vibrate in their drawers.
There is so   much danger lying around
with my infant   swaddled on the floor.
Maybe   it's the baby or the old me
who stalks   each evening on the hunt
for a sharp   pencil, a hot kiss,
my blouse   of gossamer fabric. Or maybe
it's a real ghost   let in at the threshold
that pregnancy made   of my body.
A ghost   is one more thing   to take care of
or maybe be just what I need: an excuse
to bare my teeth to   the winter darkness,
set a match to the pilot lights   in my skull,
to finally prove   who the real monster is.

Maw

When I was new to sex, I wanted to open
my boyfriend's chest like a bulkhead door.

His rusted scent, his diet of late night
diner coffee and cigarettes, to kiss him

was insufficient. It was the body horror
of first love: his near-man weight in the darkness

as his heart knocked against my head
like a speed bag. I sat in Composition

with sparks seething from my palms. Physics
tells us that between two atoms we find

near infinite empty space. Philosophy, that no one
can traverse the vastness between self and other.

When my boyfriend broke his hand
punching the locker next to my face,

I thought the two of us were getting somewhere.
I was lonely everywhere, tired of my one body

slouching across the bright linoleum. I wanted
complete, bloody entanglement, our teeth and hair,

our tongues undoing the clasps of our being.
Now my daughter climbs my chest and cuts her teeth

on my jaw. She already emptied herself
from our enmeshment, but she fights it

like any daughter of mine. I jinxed her
with this. She must learn the art

of detachment when it is already done.

Marriage

I say, *Come on*. You step
into the bathroom's yellow light

to kneel before the wound
at the base of my spine.

Black and red as a pool of wine,
there is no end to it,

like a second mouth, the one
that does half my talking,

that spoke behind my lips
in our wedding vows.

Double-voiced as a ranunculus,
we kissed you together,

a blood rush to the surface.
Now, you face it each morning

and each night until it finishes
its slow inner stitching.

You tuck a length of gauze
as clean and white as a veil

inside, so delicately that my mother
who kneels beside you says, *He is so gentle*.

You take over. The work
has become yours.

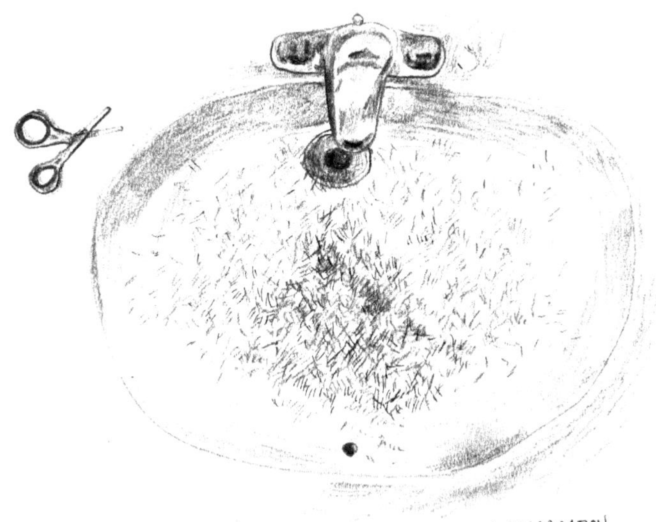

IN PREPARATION
FOR RETURNING TO WORK,
BRANDON TRIMMED HIS BEARD
LAST NIGHT. IT WAS THE
FIRST TIME HE'D DONE THAT
SINCE MINNIE'S BIRTH. THESE
HAIRS ARE MINNIE'S-LIFE LONG.

Entrails

Why must she wake up hungry again, caught arhythmic
of her mother's body, gorged and purging thimbles, soaked
through the layers of swaddle and onesie and midnight?

And why, too, does the cat, who has never warmed
to the child and her mewling, slink from its rest
and vomit into the wide set floorboards?

Haven't we seen this all before? Worn down
by her own hand in late hours, hot
and waning with tequila and television?

Wasn't she preparing then for what happens now?

And is it right that when the baby is clean
and asleep, the mother gets on her hands and knees
to clear the cat sick from between the boards
with a Q-tip, sprays down the floor so the room
stings with damp and vinegar?

Shouldn't someone call the police or the local chapter
of witches to make a report that starts with the stink
off the flannel robe the mother has been wearing
for an untold fraction of time?

Where is the record anywhere of the extinguished
firework in the mother's body, the rage she feels
over a completely ordinary awful not yet transformed
into a joke?

Or is telling anyone like a dream that evaporates
its meaning by morning or in the face
of questions like, *Isn't this what you asked for?*

Submerged

Before I was here, I was driving along the edge
of Pine Key in Florida. Along the bridges and highways,
I passed a square of dark water carved out of the island.
Slick walls, tangles of sargassum and inkberry,
it was a void where fish like black drum
and white grunt churned current as slivers
of dream. I lowered in, swam in it, and the full cool
swallowed me entirely. How I miss being wet and bright,
surrounded by strangers, crossing through gates
dark as Avernus. It was a brief moment before the water
on the other end shifted and broke in a broad curve
like the tail of fate lashing. I watched, alert, alive as asters,
as an unseen force cast a flock of birds into the air. Then
I climbed, fast and quiet, out of the water and drove
to the center of the island where the coral bed was arid
as the moon. The moon, is that where I live now?
The floor is open and spare, the air still for so long.

THERE IS AN EDGE TO OUR DAYS & A VAST QUIET

LIKE A STILL SEA. I FORGET TO DRINK WATER & THIRST

BECOMES A KIND OF MADNESS.

Seen the kettle

was all filled up

with tears

Catcall

A man in a long black t-shirt walks a slow arc
across the library lawn and calls to me:
You're a good mother. His eyes say
that he wants me to be his woman,
his mother. With this catcall as with all others,
I hate to admit how much I like it.

Last week I closed myself in the bathroom
to brush my short hair while she screamed
and scratched at the door. I didn't look in the mirror.
I waited to open the door. I understand
why a woman would wear red lipstick without
occasion, how she starts with a six pack

of Michelob Ultra and a boyfriend she met
at the Shell station to drive into a pried open night.
I dream of the Sonoran Desert, the dry path to the Pacific,
the stars overhead thickening with light. So I give
myself over to this stranger on the library lawn
for two syllables, *thank you*, and mean it.

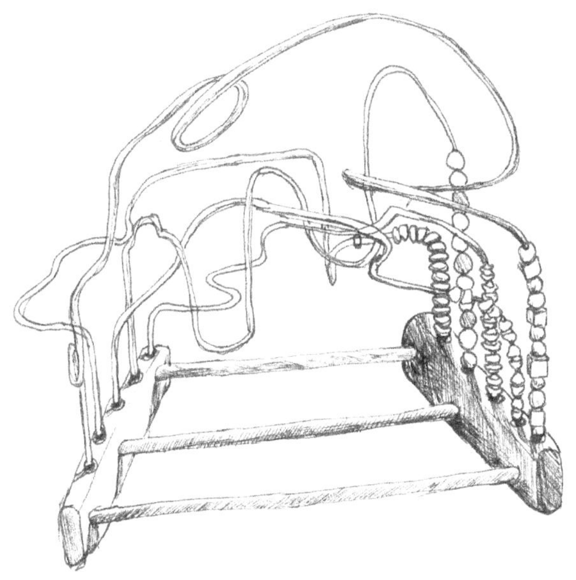

Forsythia

Once in springtime, dandelions nodding along the path,
a girl suffered a curse. When she crossed the threshold
of her kitchen like crossing a sidewalk crack, her mother
changed from the smoke of her cooking and believed the
girl was pregnant.

The daffodils said it was the boy she led to the house
or the burn of her 17th year, but whatever the cause,
the mother interrogated her daughter each morning
and every afternoon demanding to know
what the girl carried besides sorrow.

In the grave of night, the mother would wake
her daughter to ask again and refused to hear
her daughter's refusals, telling her, *You have broken*
my certainties like earthenware. I have never felt worse.

The two remained there together: voices in the dark,
their home a bunker where they breathed the same
stale air, an old, tired danger shuffling between them.
One night the mother grasped the girl's belly
beneath the spout of a running bath, hissed, *What is this?*
It was either the first sin: pregnancy or the second:
weight. In her grip, the world did and did not end.

The memory opens its yellow eyes as the girl, now

a mother herself, feels her bones light up like forsythia
branches. It is spring again. The mother's mistake
was not the hold she took of the girl. It was never claiming
what powers the curse gave her: shapeshifting, meanness,
the will to strike.

The girl was alone in her ugliness where she remained
for years. Now the baby awakens to shift in the shade.
The girl wants to protect her child, unsure as to whether
she is free. All around them the terrible trees
the city planted are flowering. There is no
escaping their sour, bright scent.

A Note to Say

that I see how your hands reach for touching.
You want dirty talk. I have a list of chores
I have completed and whatever is still to be done.

There is the fist of burp cloths and the slow
unraveling of my rage after you left the soup I made
on the counter last night, so we had to throw it out.

I am hiding in the bathroom to breathe fire
and read a news article on the toilet.
My love, it is about cave paintings.

Anthropologists measured the handprints
on cave walls and discovered both women
and children's hands flashing in ochre, umber, maroon.

I cry a little because I keep falling for it—
the old puppetry of the artist with his lone flame
licking up the walls, the imagined assault

on the sacred that the mundane presents.
The line drawn from their hands to this note twangs.
I wish we could see it all: the notches in the femur,

the knives in the rafters, the child splaying her hand
as an elder steadies the bone and blows pigment
through and onto a shoulder of rock.

Then maybe you would see it: all I have done
in the cave that caring and sickness has made of this house
where I tally everything, including forgiving you.

WHEN I PICK UP MY DAUGHTER, IT SURPRISES ME WHEN MY HANDS DON'T PASS THROUGH HER LIKE SHE'S A HOLOGRAM PROJECTED BY THE SPECIAL EFFECTS DEPARTMENT. ALL THREE DIMENSIONS, VOLUME, SURFACE AREA, FLESH & BLOOD CRY IN THE MIDDLE OF THE NIGHT. 'YES, I'M YOUR MOTHER,' I CAN SAY WOODENLY LIKE I'M READING OFF A SCRIPT. AT THE END OF THE DAY, NO ONE YELLS CUT & MY BABY WON'T DISAPPEAR INTO THE PROPMASTER'S TRUNK. AND YET, WHEN I'M AT THE GROCERY STORE, PAUSED IN THE ROAR OF THE COFFEE GRINDER, I ALMOST DON'T BELIEVE IN HER. IT'S LIKE SHE'S THE GRAND CANYON. I'VE CROSSED THE DESERT TO LOOK OUT OVER THAT BRIGHT ABYSS AND REACHED OUT MY HAND. I EXPECTED THAT MY FINGERS WOULD BOUNCE OFF THE PAINTED SCRIM AND MY TOUCH WOULD THUNDER DOWN ITS FLAT FALSENESS. IT TOO WAS UNBELIEVABLE, HUGE, HUED LIKE A 1950'S POSTCARD, SOMETHING I WAS TOLD I WOULD LOVE AND DID IMMEDIATELY & DRUNKENLY AS A TOURIST. IT BURNED TO LOOK AT THE VASTNESS. WHAT DID THE LAND BELIEVE AS THE RIVER CUT INTO IT? THERE IS NO HISTORY OF SKEPTICISM AS THE COLORADO OPENED THE ROCK EVER WIDER & EVER DEEPER. AND THERE WAS THE EARTH IN LAYERED RIBBONS OF MAUVE, TAUPE, & BRICK, REVEALED & ASTONISHING, UNCOMPREHENDING AS SHE BECAME ANOTHER EARTH ALTOGETHER.

Actress

A woman who came to acting late in life was asked
if she could cry on stage. Her reply: *Oh my dear,*
if you need me to, I could cry and cry and cry.

When I wanted to be an actress,
I was told to conjure my oldest hates and pains
in the wings. In theory, when I stepped out
from behind the curtain, I would run
that molten metal straight through the lines
and fuel a stranger's heart on it.

But I was 19 and afraid. I jumped and huffed
and tried to yell, felt an almost-feeling,
a half-fury, like when my first boyfriend
would tell me to come.

I wish I had known to use the fear.
There was so much of it. And now,
of course, it's all over.

I wander the apartment under a lagging spotlight,
spilling everywhere, stitching
a quilted monologue out of breakfast.
There is no offstage, only a makeshift costume
of unconvincing calm. Alone,

I am the shocked audience. I scream
into the flat face of the steering wheel
on the way to pick up more baby Tylenol,
more teething gel. Tonight,
I could eat Lady Macbeth.

19 Months in Quarantine

The man down the street hurls the contents
of his first floor apartment onto the sidewalk.
The cops keep coming back as his stuff contracts
in and out of his house: a tossed ream

of construction paper slapped flat with rain,
the traffic cone he stuck on the parking sign
like a dunce cap. We go on walks and steer
the stroller around half his orange couch, the belch

of its stuffing on the greenway. This is our place
in the animal kingdom. Our neighbor is a jester,
his art, a gesture of colorful madness and waste.
The forest skirts the neighborhood but doesn't

know us. We had to inform the state a few days
after your birth when I wanted more to tell
the tulip bulbs. In our limited wilderness, I wait
for you to speak. I speak my thoughts aloud that you

may hear the general melody of language. I taught you
sign language for your small wants, *milk, please, more.*
I ask questions, and you take on the wise vacancy
of a fawn I once found while walking a fence line. God

makes perfect creatures and lays them in a spiral
of woven grass the same way I lay you

on the blue rug printed with pansies. Your silence
is the silence of violets. I enter your stare like a room

made of sky. I believe that you know something
of the fragile planet, the flint of the soul, something
leftover from your time in the darkness.
The knowledge recedes. We'll never catch it.

I take you to the corner and point to all the colors
our neighbor left behind. Purple, brown, green,
green, green. You bunch your fingertips
and tap them together, *more, more.*

Oracle

It is said that the oracle at Delphi
offered her prophecies in an utter fever.

Intoxicated on fumes from a split in the rock,
she inhaled and babbled in pearl-eyed hysteria
like the future had warped her mind.

But history is littered with rumor.
She could have spoken in her own voice,
quiet and even. I imagine

the silence that followed her proclamations
sounded like our neighborhood
past midnight where any one of us turns
desperate before the glow of our phones,

drunk on loneliness asking questions like,
am I pregnant? how much blood
is too much blood?
why can't I feel the baby?
what if my baby hates me?
what if I hate myself?

A flat oracle, the cold light,
the homesick notion that anyone is there
to answer us. A friend took
the abortion pill and in the rare caul

of her broken heart googled,
did it work? did it work?
There's a horror and a hope that maybe
it didn't. The Eleusinian mysteries

of our own bodies: how a heartbeat survives
or doesn't, the absolute silence.
Our questions echo back to us on WebMD,
a new elder with more answers and no love.

The oracle at Delphi was called Pythia,
a translation of *to rot*, the sickening sweetness
of decay or the film of wine
in the empty glass at the bedside.

Nights like this happen for everyone, don't they?
Before the baby, after the baby,
the algorithms hum their mysterious songs.

In its clean vapors, I am the baby now,
half asleep in shrouded frenzy,
lost as the old gods.

I KNEW THE SNOW WAS COMING WHEN THE LIGHT WENT BONE-BLUE. I WRITE IN THE FLUTTERING DARKNESS THAT FOLLOWS AFTER I BEND TO MY CHILD WEARILY, POSTURE LIKE PICASSO'S OLD GUITARIST. MY HUSBAND ALREADY CURVES THIS WAY TOO AT THE END OF THE BED, READY TO LIFT HER INTO THE COLD COBALT AIR. THESE ARE THE HOURS FOR WHICH PICASSO PAINTED HIS BLUE PERIOD, WHERE THE NIGHT ACHES FROM BUFFETING WINDS, A HUNGRY CHILD THAT WON'T EAT. I SAW THOSE PAINTINGS ONCE, IN BOSTON, AS A CHILD. I HURRIED THROUGH THE GALLERIES, ONLY
SLOWING DOWN WHEN I FOUND THEM, CANVASES THE COLOR OF NEW BREASTMILK, EARLY WINTER, & MIDNIGHT. MY MOTHER CAUGHT UP TO ME & TOOK HOLD OF THE FAT ON THE BACK OF MY ARM, "YOU NEED TO STOP." THE RAGE SHE FELT THEN STILL CHILLS ME NOW AS I SIT ALONE IN THE ROCKER WILLING MY DAUGHTER QUIET & ASLEEP. NOW I UNDERSTAND, AS I TIGHTEN HER SWADDLE, THE LIFELONG TEETH OF MOTHERHOOD: YOU TEAR LOOSE A WILD DESIRE, THEN STRIVE EVERY HOUR TO CONTAIN IT. EVEN IN SLEEP, SHE ESCAPES
MY HANDS.

Sacred cow

When we lined the herd along the wall and settled
their heads in the stanchions, the farmer brought
the lever down to secure them in a line. I often
had to leap back from the swing of their heads.
Whether it was the bony, temperamental architecture
of the Holsteins or the amiable Brown Swiss,
they contained the kind of power once named in rituals.
They moved around me as slowly as mothers around
their children. Now they were trapped in a row,
and the vet moved amongst them steadily as a priest
down the long aisle between pews.

He reached shoulder deep into each one, sweeping
his hand into the darkness of them. Every cow
would be tested for motherhood for it was the season.
By feel, he measured the thickness and tilt
of each cervix, the liquid bulge of each
uterine horn heavy with calf.

A loose one strayed beyond our reach. She was gold
and ornery. Her hooves clattered away from us
on the stone floor. We cornered her over a thatch
of hay, and the vet did his work. I don't remember
if she was pregnant or not, but I do recall the rage
in her glare like that of Hera, Hathor, my own mother
when I talked back and all her burdens rose up
before her as enemies.

Her anger is a memory and a familiar raiment
both terrible and glorious. I swing my head around
the room while my child tugs at the pocket
of my sweatpants, climbs my legs as I pour the milk.
I cannot rest, broad and tired
and entirely forfeited into another's hands.

Black and white

A cage cam at the zoo
caught footage
of a panda mother lost
in thought, stripping
a hunk of bamboo
with her teeth.
She startles
and quickly sets
her paws down to hook
her big head around
and look for her cub.
I was warned that I
would forget the twins
I miscarried in the face
of my living child,
and I do.
I startle when
I remember them
and look around
as though they lived.
She and I both find
our children
exactly where they are.

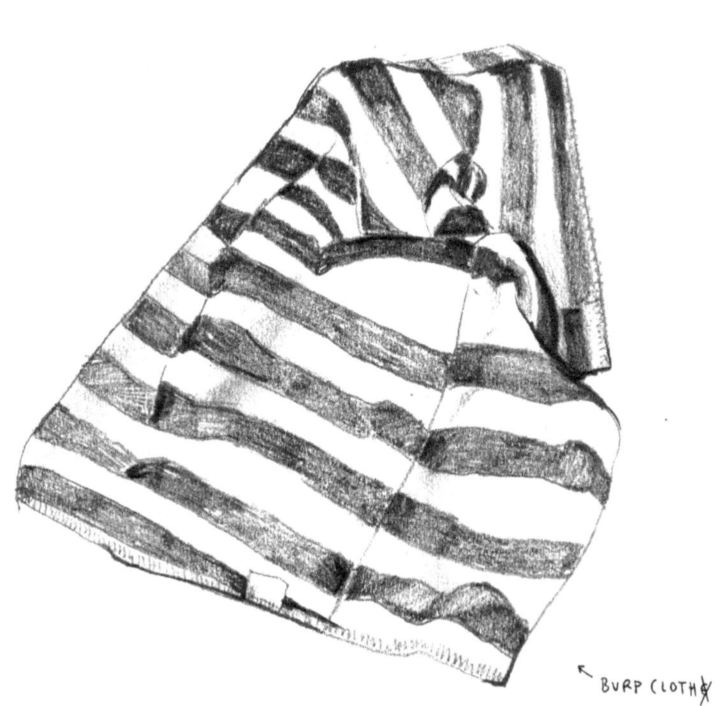
BURP CLOTH

Old Friend

In the gloom of the root cellar
its eyes click open. It comes
when its called, a hound,
a bone head fronting a red machine.

I remember from my childhood,
the long hot POV shot burning through
the film reel. There was no funeral

to mark the death of mine,
just a slow throw
of soil over its mouth.

My daughter spent months in the dark of me
where she acquainted herself with whatever
I'd shuttered in my gut.
I felt her in there digging around.

Often when I say, *no,*
not now, not that, my girl goes

blank-faced and gets out my old claws,
grasps fast at my hair, throws
stones like a zealot scalded with god.

A bark of laughter fists in the throat.
I swallow it so that I may eat my joy.
My rage, I am happy
to see you again.

Mother of Thousands

He climbed the stairs with a fistful of seedlets,
their hair-thin roots already reaching, dirt,
and a terracotta pot in the dead of midwinter.
We undress. He wet the earth and taught me
where to guide the seeds into it. That week,
I was sore from clinging to him. To him
it was good sense that after sex on my sunken mattress,
after a dinner of flaking fish and pickled onions,
we'd dirty our hands planting.

He called the seedlings mother of thousands,
though they have more sinister names:
alligator plant, devil's backbone. It felt right
like what he saw in me: a mother and a vice entwined.
I wanted that, to be wanted badly.

Today when I knocked over the pot, it fractured.
I set our daughter down, untangle the roots
and replant the mother. Fresh earth
will restore it after the throttle of the fall.
A thousand more seeds line its leaves
like the thousand yeses I've been
handing over since he arrived
at my door ready for something.

Handing Down

I sit on the floor in front of my daughter's
baby saucer and eat cold forkfuls of pork
and cabbage. I let her watch as hunger
works over me.

My grandmother used to smooth
whipped cream over a walnut cake then
close herself away to heave up its sweetness.
It kept her thin as a broom handle
and lent her a quiet glamor. Once

on a walk at dusk to gather bittersweet,
my mother said that she wished above all else
to be thin again as though fate could
be haggled with. Further back,

my great-grandmother married a man
whose own mother denied her meat
at Sunday dinner, and she ran from them both
to a house down the road that leaned west
with weeds and rust. I have been

no different. I pulled what I ate from my throat;
knobs of bread, songs of cream, I took
them back like reversing a vow, laced
my eyelids with broken blood. And now

she's here. She watches. She wants the next
bite, wants to sing the line that is to follow.

I let the rubber spoon approach her mouth.
As she grasps my thumb and pulls in,
the next hour swallows us mercilessly.

LIGHT BROKEN
THROUGH BLACK LOCUST BRANCHES,
MY DAUGHTER'S
FACE KEEPS
DISAPPEARING.
Bunny

Condition

Motherhood has made me unhappy.
I am familiar with unhappiness.
It is an uncanny companion. I met it
as a child when my father bellowed
down the stairs in the same voice
that his father used on him
or when me and the neighbor kids
were called in from the dusk.
I've met it in classrooms,
in my bed, in other people's beds,
while drunk or sober as a saint,
or full to the gills with Thanksgiving turkey.
I met it on the radiating blacktop
outside the Hyatt in Phoenix, Arizona
and more of it in the lobby
where a throng of intense,
humorless young professionals
were doing important things in starched slacks
while I stood stupefied in a wilted summer dress.
I was to join them for my first "real" job,
and I hated them all.
Unhappiness regularly joins me at the dentist.
Unhappiness became the third wheel
in the last relationship I had
before your father, the one with the man
who hung his head as I walked in the door,
whose pained expression over dinner,
his disappointment at I-don't-know-what,

made me exhaust myself guessing.
There was an almost comfortable monotony
of the wrongness of that relationship
and many others before.
Your mother has known crystalline,
utterly clear moments of unhappiness.
They kept me alive. I kept them
until I became bored of them.
But the unhappiness of motherhood,
like its happiness, continually refreshes itself
with new teeth, new tastes,
and new dangers. I love
to choose it every day
when I wake up.
I pray each night that
I will never be free
of it, its metamorphic harm.

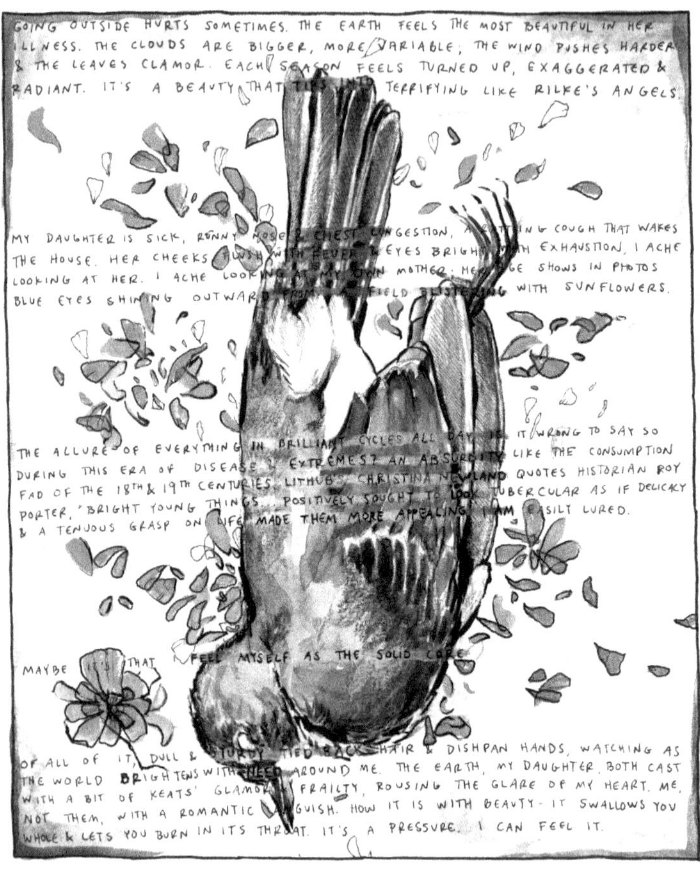
GOING OUTSIDE HURTS SOMETIMES. THE EARTH FEELS THE MOST BEAUTIFUL IN HER
ILLNESS. THE CLOUDS ARE BIGGER, MORE VARIABLE; THE WIND PUSHES HARDER
& THE LEAVES CLAMOR. EACH SEASON FEELS TURNED UP, EXAGGERATED &
RADIANT. IT'S A BEAUTY THAT TIPS INTO TERRIFYING LIKE RILKE'S ANGELS.
MY DAUGHTER IS SICK, RUNNY NOSE & CHEST CONGESTION, A RATTLING COUGH THAT WAKES
THE HOUSE. HER CHEEKS FLUSH WITH FEVER & EYES BRIGHT WITH EXHAUSTION. I ACHE
LOOKING AT HER. I ACHE LOOKING AT MY OWN MOTHER. HER IMAGE SHOWS IN PHOTOS
BLUE EYES SHINING OUTWARD FROM A FIELD BLISTERING WITH SUNFLOWERS.
IS IT WRONG TO SAY SO
THE ALLURE OF EVERYTHING IN BRILLIANT CYCLES ALL DAY. LIKE THE CONSUMPTION
DURING THIS ERA OF DISEASE & EXTREMES? AN ABSURDITY QUOTES HISTORIAN ROY
FAD OF THE 18TH & 19TH CENTURIES. LITHUB'S CHRISTINA NEWLAND
PORTER, 'BRIGHT YOUNG THINGS... POSITIVELY SOUGHT TO LOOK TUBERCULAR AS IF DELICACY
& A TENUOUS GRASP ON LIFE MADE THEM MORE APPEALING.' I AM EASILY LURED.
MAYBE IT'S THAT I FEEL MYSELF AS THE SOLID CORE
OF ALL OF IT, DULL & STURDY, TIED BACK HAIR & DISHPAN HANDS, WATCHING AS
THE WORLD BRIGHTENS WITH NEED AROUND ME. THE EARTH, MY DAUGHTER, BOTH CAST
WITH A BIT OF KEATS' GLAMOR & FRAILTY, ROUSING THE GLARE OF MY HEART. ME,
NOT THEM, WITH A ROMANTIC ANGUISH. HOW IT IS WITH BEAUTY - IT SWALLOWS YOU
WHOLE & LETS YOU BURN IN ITS THROAT. IT'S A PRESSURE. I CAN FEEL IT.

Cut

I shred my knuckles
with the cheese grater, split
the space between two fingers
with a retracting tape measure.
Nothing is continuous anymore.
I recover and recover.
In every room, my eye lingers
on edges, the fate that waits
to unfold from a forgotten pair
of scissors. I count the marks
on my daughter. I caught her
neck in the zipper of her onesie,
pinched her fingertip in a dollhouse door.
Her skin is a brail of my failures.
Each day, I find the will to spare
her more and more. All other wills
are spent. Where is the hand
to hold my own falling head?

I WANT TO HOLD HER THE WAY

THE WORLD SHOULD

I have lost

one of the LOOSELY,

CAREFULLY,

GRIP OPENING OVER YEARS

Excavator

Houses shake with excavation. With a low shuddering
like tremors of memory, I bring my head to order.

We need a lunch break. If only I had a union leader,
a builder of coalitions who could translate the charisma

of my larynx or the embattled genius of my liver
to the tyranny of the brain, we could come to an accord:

a regular hour of rest, a permanent forgiveness.
But I am no radical. I walk my daughter around

the corner where big machines dig up half the street.
When we sit, I show her the five goldfish in my palm.

She hollers with want. The pistons of my heart
are automatic, but my body has followed trends

to become a hustle culture, a gig economy,
giving it up at all hours and under any condition.

Before us, a huge scaffold bakes on the street.
It will be settled beneath the pavement and put

to its mysterious work, and the kids on Elmwood
will never know it's there. She won't remember

this morning or the kindly construction workers
or my cupful of topless strawberries. One day,

she will feel it— bitterness, warmth, my mothering—
as it flutters its pages, an aging manual. Later today,

I will call to wish my own mother a Happy Birthday.
Such a well-used mechanism should whir between us

with insect efficiency, but I have often failed to engineer
her joy. Blame my poor spatial sense or the strangeness

of what things look like flipped over. What wore her
down when I was there but untrained? I envy

the excavator. A clank and hush and all is unearthed.
Yes, the delved-in earth, its scent of musk and metal.

Instead, we have chisels. I mean, children.

ALGORITHM

My brain runs its algorithms:
listing escape routes
or packing suitcases
for the unimaginable landscape of rest.
To die sounds like another ceaseless task.
I have too many bones, too much flesh.
For all my parts, I can't burden
anyone with the leftovers.
For now, I'm the one that cleans up
the messes. My hands are the hands
that clap in the dark and wash dishes
like pale sorcerer's gloves.
Who fills the gloves that grip
the broom? A shadowy thick
slowness, an exhaustion
that keeps the rent paid. And yet
I think that Brandon still has time
to find another wife.
In one last vibrant burst of energy,
I can be replaced
by other hands, another tit,
and my daughter, for whom
all the curves and softness of this world
are new and interchangeable,
might not notice. You see?
It is only when I am this bad
that I feel worth killing.

ONCE HUNG UP ON
A GUY WHO WOULDN'T
TEXT ME BACK &
A BIT WINE DRUNK
BEHIND THE WHEEL
(I AM ASHAMED TO
SAY), I MISCALCULATED
THE SPEED & DISTANCE
OF A MASSIVE,
BRILLIANTLY LIT TRUCK
ON ROUTE 7. I PULLED
OUT AHEAD OF IT &
FELT ITS GRAVITY SO
CLOSE IT COULD HAVE
DRAGGED ME INTO ITS
CHROME GRILL, THE
NARROW SPACE BETWEEN
US. THE SHUDDERING
JOLT OF MY FUTURE
SPLITTING IN TWO.
ON ONE THREAD, I
LIVED & LIVE HERE
STILL, 11 YEARS DEEP
IN THIS TOWN, HAVING
LONG LOST THAT MAN'S
PHONE NUMBER. ON
THE OTHER, I DIE,
SMASHED TO COMPLETE
ANNIHILATION IN MY
RED SCION. THE FRAIL
SEAM THAT LEADS
ME TO BRANDON TEARS
~~COLLAPSES~~ & YEARS
LATER, HE LEAVES
VERMONT ALTOGETHER.
MINNIE CRACKLES
OUT OF POSSIBILITY.
EACH SECOND, 4-5
BABIES ARE BORN
& 1-2 PEOPLE DIE.
THAT NIGHT, AFTER
AN EVENING OF
BOARD GAMES WITH
FRIENDS OF FRIENDS,
CHECKING MY
PHONE & SNEAKING
"JUST A HALF-
GLASS MORE"
OF WINE
I TURNED ONTO
THE DARK ROAD,
THE FULL WEIGHT
OF THE TRUCK
RUSHING PAST & FELT
MYSELF VANISH IN
SOME OTHER PLACE.
MINNIE HAS THIS TOY,
AN OLD ONE OF HER
FATHER'S - A LITTLE
PLASTIC MAN IN A RED
SHIRT & BLUE PANTS,
A BLUE BASEBALL CAP
FOREVER FASTENED TO
HIS HEAD. WHEN YOU
PULL THE STRING AT HIS
FEET, HE STRAIGHTENS
UP. WHEN YOU LET GO,
HE COLLAPSES. BRANDON
SAID TO HER, KNOWING
SHE WON'T REMEMBER,
"CAN YOU BELIEVE
THAT IS WHAT'S INSIDE
EVERYONE - JUST A LONG
YELLOW STRING HOLDING
US UP?" & I SAID, "YES,
& ONE DAY, GOD
LETS GO." I HAD
TO SURVIVE MYSELF
SO MANY TIMES TO
GET HERE - LONG,
DARK ROADS, BOTTLES,
THE WRONG END OF
UNKIND MEN & MY
OWN SAD HEART, ALL
METHODS OF PLAYING
TUG-OF-WAR WITH
THE ROPE OF MY FATE,
DARING IT TO GO
SLACK IN MY HANDS.
I DRIVE MORE SLOWLY
NOW, STONE SOBER,
SIT STILL FOR HOURS
& DELAY MY DEATH
FOR AS LONG AS I CAN
SO I MAY REMAIN
HERE WITH THEM, MY
DAUGHTER & HUSBAND

Mercy

My daughter licks the icing
from a pumpkin-shaped cookie
then demands that I eat the rest.
A spiced Eucharist,
damp with her spit,
crumbles on my tongue.
Meals, cakes, cookies dissolve
down my bloodline. Hunger
diffuses amongst the heavy women
in my family but never disappears.
We flagellate. We thrash with hate
on the small dark altars of our hearts.
My daughter, a little curate,
consecrates everything
she feeds me. In the deep red
wine of midmorning,
I drink. I eat.

Close

a classroom of girls dancing around bowls
of fire at their feet, their dark hair swinging

the scent of linden in a forest in June

a child you don't know who asks you to sit and comfort
her on the cold linoleum, who repairs the wounds
of her losses in your arms

a broth so braided with flavor
that you believe you are loved

even at my thickest, the dimmest
of my wit, I know what it is

my feathered hours sing their length
the clocks slow by an untold measure
time is replenished
as it is spent in vast tides

TO REMEMBER THAT
I WANT
TO WITNESS
I AM HERE
EVERYTHING THAT HAPPENS IN THE FACE
OF FEAR & WHAT CAN BE
PRESERVED

Confession

No church, just a river of incense
passing through me from
an unseen starting place.

In its absence, I had a swingset,
rituals of song and quiet, felt drunk
on the light through birch leaves.

I burned with awe back then. Still do
when white lilacs drop their musk
from the branches,

branches that quake and shatter
as though speaking in tongues.
I confessed it all

to the mesh of moth webs overhead.
For tales, I had the abridged Bible
Nana bought me at the surplus store.

It was illustrated with Precious Moments children,
eyes pinched into weepy tear shapes
by what they saw: open wounds,

passage across the desert through
nets of bandits. The closest thing
to comfort was the mother

who would rather give up her child
than halve her with a sword. The armor
of angels, the vestments,

gold-flung ecstasies immortalized in sculpture,
I've been told the sacred lives there and in bread
and the gem-encrusted skulls of saints.

Behind St. Joseph's Cathedral
I shortcut toward town. In my pocket, I carry
a plastic Grover that my daughter gave me at dropoff.

I trace small prayers for her and the rest of us
over this little blue relic. A young man
sits alone beneath a tree,

head bowed. It's morning, and I hope his god
is nearby. My own is like an old flame.
We never speak, but we think

of one another in winces and turns.
If I stay very still and breathe in the blacktop
shadow of the church, I will catch fire.

Matter

In the heavy shade of the nursery,
she lets herself be lifted, cleaned, and clothed
before I pour her somnolent body into her crib.
The word matter comes from *materia*
as in timber or substance, the stuff of this living world,
but before that, from *mater* or mother. My matter,
her mother, is the substance of her, the timbre
of my voice molding her first darknesses. I opened
my eyes again today. She grips
the hem of my garment.

THE WORD ONEIRIC KEEPS APPEARING IN MY READING. FROM THE GREEK ONEIROS, IT MEANS
ANYTHING RELATED DREAMS OR DREAMING. MORE THAN ONE AUTHOR WANTS ME TO THINK
ABOUT DREAM THINGS. MOST OF MY LIFE THIS YEAR HAS BEEN A DREAM. NOT DREAMY IN
THE CANDY CANE WAY WE TEND TO SAY, THOUGH MOTHERHOOD HAS GIVEN ME MOMENTS
OF UNBEARABLE SWEETNESS. MORE IN THE HAZY WAY, THE STANDING-IN-THE-NURSERY-
FORGETTING-HOW-I-GOT-THERE WAY, THE FORGETTING-WHAT-I'M-SAYING MIDSENTENCE WAY.
WHAT A MONSTROUS EFFORT IT TAKES TO RECALL THE RECENT PAST, TO GATHER IT UP &
MAKE SENSE OF IT. CONSTANTLY I ASK MYSELF, "WHAT AM I DOING?" I SEE WHAT
ISN'T THERE (LITTLE BLACK FLAGS IN THE PERIPHERY), HEAR WHAT'S NEVER UTTERED (MY
NAME, MY DAUGHTER'S CRIES), & THERE'S ALWAYS A SONG PLAYING IN MY HEAD THAT
BECOMES MANIACAL BY REPETITION. ALL DAY, A LONG DREAM I NEVER WAKE FROM,
BUT LEARN TO NAVIGATE. MINNIE'S LEARNING HOW TO WALK. SHE MOVES LIKE SHE'S
STEPPING OVER INVISIBLE CLOUDS, UNSTEADY & TUMBLING. BUT SHE DOESN'T WORRY
ABOUT IT. SHE RISES AGAIN & AGAIN, ARCHES HERSELF INTO BALANCE & CROSSES
THE LIVING ROOM TO HARASS THE HOUSEPLANT. MEANWHILE, I FALL ALL THE TIME. EACH
MOMENT, A SMALL CASCADE, INTO NEW SLEEP, TO BED, TO THE COUCH, TO THE FLOOR TO
WATCH MINNIE THROW BLOCKS AROUND. HERE WE ARE, IN THE FALL, ITS THINNESS
BETWEEN STATES OF BEING (WAKING/SLEEPING, WARM/COLD, LIFE/DEATH) BEFORE THE
DESCENT OF WINTER. EVERYTHING IS ONEIRIC NOW—ALIVE & SYMBOLIC & LOOSE. I NEED
AN ORACLE TO READ ME MY LIFE OR TO ACCEPT, FINALLY, MY UNDONE CONTROL & FLOAT ON.

Return

There was once a man who walked the dim hours between
night and day. Three strides behind him
walked his mother and in his mother's arms,
his infant son. The man carried his old sorrows
and stories and memories, like that of his brother
whom cancer had taken young.

Families knot backwards into one another. When one
dies, the globe of a mother ripens and a new baby arrives
to replace who was lost. Or even restore, as was the case
with this man, whose brother stepped into the darkness
then turned back. When the man's wife became pregnant,
the man suspected they would have a son.

Indeed a son was born, and the man recognized
his brother immediately—a crease in the sole of his foot,
the smallness of his ears, and the broad forehead behind
which the stories of many lives resided briefly before
lifting into silence under the fluorescent hospital light.

Now the man walks the neighborhood, the proud father
of his brother, balding with joy and exhaustion.
The audience of his neighbors suffers a reluctant doubt.
They listen, nod, encourage their own children
to flap their chubby arms at his brother-son.

They want everything he says to be true: that we never
lose anyone, that we pass through time with a collection
of souls netted to us, that our dead wait to circle back
to the neighborhood of the living. What a relief it would be

to know that the pull we feel is not only the rhythm
of our own time, but of all time and of them, urging us
forward until it is our turn to be carried.

Forgetting

A daughter is a reminder—
the old fears of childhood
where toy fire trucks are lined up
at the threshold like sentries
and even the kitchen can become sinister
when night falls. The half-moon
of my daughter's eye is always turned
toward the ancient woods. She remembers
that there are bigger beasts.
A leashless dog bounds out from the brush
and shakes his stupid head at her.
As the color retreats from her face
so she looks lunar, obscured,
her scream is the siren of primal children.
Her dread feels out of step with the warning labels
on her baby bath, her swaddles stitched
with patches that warn *back is best*
but it isn't. They are the same.
Her screams and my foreboding
are a translation of the years before
I was taught and she will be taught
to fight the speed of fear in her brain,
the jangling alarms of her nerves.
Death is there. She knows it.
I know it. Her growing up
is an act of forgetting.

Lightning

The trees roar sideways
as the storm digs its elbows
into the grass, circles

the house like an animal.
How many times have we
done this, disrobed

at the keen edge
of lightning, the spark
you strike in my teeth

with your tongue? You
circled me all morning,
waiting for our daughter

to fall asleep. From the darkness
in her room, all of it—
my cries, the bed's ache—sounds

like a smooth rush of rain.
She never stirs in her sleep.

Ignis Fatuus

The rain starts slowly. I let the baby
sleep and push her around the thrift store.
Persian rugs, brass door pulls,
smoky cocktail glasses, in each corner
lies furnished visions of a different life
from the one I've chosen.
As the patter on the roof quiets,
I roll her outside to the edge
of the property where the flat mud
rings a wetland. Racks of rust,
train tracks, boxcars in a line
and then, the lake. There
are hymns out there that hover
like swamp lights.
I hear the purr of one beyond
the hush of grass and gravel.
They are there. And there.
They wait for me.

Ground Cherries

AFTER JAMES WRIGHT

On my knees at the raised bed, I crouch
to harvest ground cherries. In the long summer
their stalks grow thick as wrists, their husks
pale with age. At the moment
of absolute ripeness, their stems relent.
They fall to the earth where we find them
and peel back the thinning sheath
to a perfectly smooth fruit inside,
tourmaline and tart. In the long grass
my daughter spirals around the garden,
and asks for more in broken speech.
She bites the brightness from its skin.
It is here, the air in early evening
clear and cool, where desire reaches
its end, a finishing. The paper
opens, a small sun rises.

Cloth Mother

We stroke lamb's wool in your board books
and practice saying, *soft, soft*. When you slap me,

I say, *show me gentle*, and you rest your open hand
on my bare shoulder, then repeat after me, *gentle*,

in doughy consonants. I have tried hard
to harden my body in preparation for the real world

that I was promised. A good woman can spit nail tack
and make an all butter crust in an apocalypse.

I try to go tough against you, a leather mother,
a wire mother, a cage where you drag

your cup against the bars. All so you will obey,
learn to wring your milk from steel. This

is how I obey or fail to. When you dig your fingernails
into my neck, I sneak you my softened voice,

think of goose feathers or bread wet with mold,
how much can grow in the rot. I say, *no, no, baby*,

after you've tossed your eggs into the carpet
with a voice round as a stone's echo in a well.

I don't know what you will become under
such downy supervision. Each night you prepare

for bed in the same way. You wind up
your little body and heave yourself into the pillow

of my underbelly, breathing deeply
like you are in love.

HER TEETH BREAKING
FRUIT
THE JUICE
THE FULL
SHUDDERING
TREES
EACH UNFINISHED
MOMENT
there.
IT ALL BECOMES SLEEP

Daughter

slaps other children's heads
right where they first hit the air of the world

scoops water with an alligator
and drinks from the toothed chalice of its mouth

drinks from a puddle constellated
with dandelion seed

fills her glittery shoes with water and drinks again

tears tomatillos in half, drops the halves
in her father's garden bed

tangles her fingers in an orb weaver's legs

clutches a bumblebee and squeezes the gold
out to smear on her pantlegs

plucks the neighbor's one open peony

fills her mouth with gravel

fills her nose with corn kernels

fills her hands with the flesh of my cheeks,
   leaves red trenches in my jaw

leaves a soggy diaper on the kitchen floor

pushes my lips into my teeth with her forehead
  until I taste a spark of blood

asks for ghost stories, dreams of skeletons in her crib,
witches cracking broomsticks on the rails

was born with cries like magnolia petals

Monument

Sometimes, while she eats,
I sit in front of her and just hold
her warm feet.

When I get out of the shower,
she slaps my sagging breasts,
pokes at my belly button,
and pats my pubic hair
and asks, *What that? What that?*
As it transforms, I want to tell her
it is a monument

like the bronze men on horseback
in the park. Battle-worn,
I like this language better
than what it has been
having been so much worse.

The hours I care for my daughter
represent a brief armistice
in an old war I resume as soon as
she goes to sleep.

She whispers to herself,
practices words she wants to know,
catta, uppy, mama,
a tender private speech.

I weep at the sink in the morning.
How can I teach her
that her love can be directed
inward, the same place
where her misgivings
and hatreds reside?

How can I teach her
what I don't know?
I feed her days one at a time.
Our only work is to go calmly,
to allow life to move
through us and beyond,

invite the sheer spread of life,
its spill. I watch as it stretches
out of my reach.

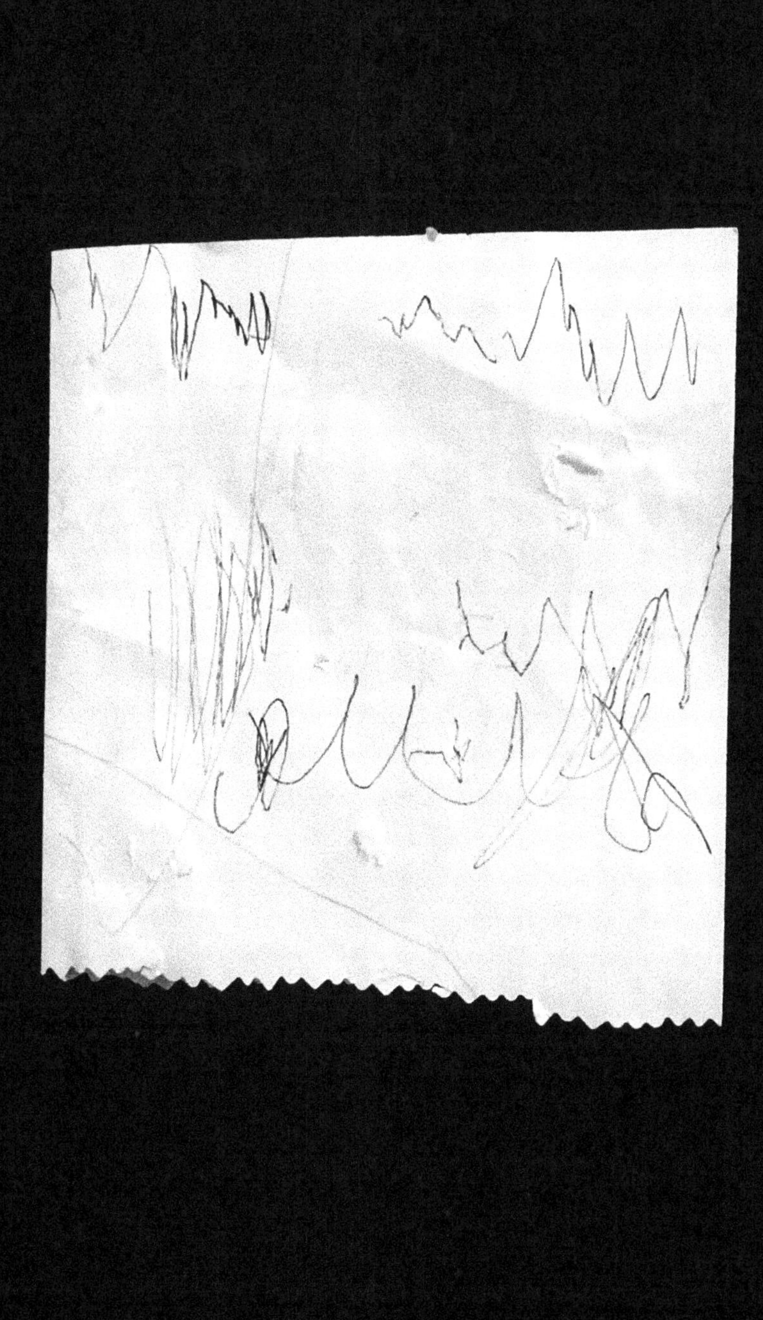

Condition Images

Scan to view images in greater detail and in color.

Notes

A number of images in this collection were drawn from the following children's books:

"Grasses" is drawn from *Days with Frog and Toad* written and illustrated by Arnold Lobel

"In and Out of Weeks" is drawn from *Where the Wild Things Are* written and illustrated by Maurice Sendak

"I Heard Something Outside My Window" is drawn from *The Bear's Toothache* written and illustrated by David McPhail

"Tear Water Tea" is drawn from *Owl at Home* written and illustrated by Arnold Lobel

"Goodnight __________" is drawn from *Goodnight Moon* written and illustrated by Margaret Wise Brown

"Button" is drawn from *Frog and Toad Are Friends* written and illustrated by Arnold Lobel

"Just Quietly" is drawn from *The Story of Ferdinand* written by Munro Leaf & illustrated by Robert Lawson

"Pony" is drawn from *Fritz and the Beautiful Horses* written and illustrated by Jan Brett

"The Mystery" is drawn from *The Mystery of the Flying Orange Pumpkin* written and illustrated by Steven Kellogg

"There" is drawn from *The Snowy Day* written and illustrated by Ezra Jack Keats

Acknowledgments

An ardent thank you to the editors of the following publications in which these poems and comics first appeared:

Maternochronics: "11 Months in Quarantine"
Seven Days: "13 Months in Quarantine"
Kenyon Review: "Plums" & "Handing Down"
New England Review: "Oracle"
Iterant: "Grand Canyon" & "Blue Period"
Shō Poetry Journal: "Milkstone"
Pleiades: "Cloth Mother"
Cordite: Poetry Review "Return"
Iron Horse Literary Review: "Bath" and "15 Months in Quarantine"
Ambient Receiver: "Sacred Cow" & "Black and White"
Funicular Magazine: "Submerged," "Collision," & "19 Months in Quarantine"
The Indianapolis Review: "Oneiric," "Rope," & "Allure of Everything"
Cottonmouth: "Marriage"

I also wish to thank Rusty Morrison for selecting my manuscript for The Hillary Gravendyk Prize and all those at the Inlandia Institute, particularly Laura Villareal and Cati Porter, for seeing this collection through to publication.

I will always thank my teachers in both my undergraduate and graduate work, Sanford Freedman, Steve Dillon, Robert Farnsworth, Robert Feintuch, Sue E. Houchins, Carol Anne Taylor, Pamela Johnson, Annie Finch, Kazim Ali, Joshua Davis, Tony Barnstone, Cait Johnson, Tim Seibles, and Sholeh Wolpe as well my fellow students, Katie Bickham, Sarah Steinberg Heller, Casey Moynihan, Penny Guisinger, Amanda Johnson,

Rooze McKelvey, Alan King, and Quenton Baker who altered my mind and expanded my heart.

I dearly thank my poetry community: Kerrin McCadden, Maria Hummel, Tanya Stone, Penelope Cray, Eve Alexandra, Jari Chevalier, Kristin Fogdall, Elizabeth Powell, Major Jackson, Didi Jackson, Alison Prine, Benjamin Aleshire, Rajnii Eddins, Holly Painter, Bill Stratton, Frances Cannon, Skye Jackson, Gennarose Nethercott, Noah Burton, Denise Casey, Leanne Ruell, Candace Jensen, Kiev Rattee, Aaron Lovett, Ruth Antoinette Rodriguez, Ben Pease, Barbara Murphy, Drew Frazier, Neil Shepard, Chard deNiord, Emer Feeney, Larissa Hebert, Bill Drislane, and Sarah Bartlett. I love you all.

Thank you, Margaret Adams and Julia C. Alter, for supporting the first draft of this manuscript and to Bethany Breitland for reading it and offering utterly priceless revision advice with your absolute acuity and brilliance.

I want to specifically thank my dear friend and the strongest woman I know, Amy Johnson, who answered every text and fielded every one of my fears in early motherhood. You continue to show me how it's done.

Also, my gratitude to Bianca Stone, who let me email her a poem every day for nine months, so I could turn the mess of my journals into poems and comics, and who continues to encourage me to push all boundaries of poetry and art. You astonish me.

Thank you to my family, Susie, Al, Justin, Julie, Jeslyn, Jansen, and Jaycie and Mom, Dad, and Al, I love you. I am very lucky.

Brandon and Minnie, you are the center of my life. Loving you is my first and greatest work.

About Inlandia Institute

The Inlandia Institute is an Inland Southern California-based literary and cultural arts non-profit and publishing house. We seek to bring focus to the richness of the literary enterprise that has existed in this region for ages.

The mission of Inlandia Books is to recognize, support, and expand literary activity in Inland Southern California by publishing works which deepen people's awareness, understanding, and appreciation of this unique, complex and creatively vibrant region. The mission is carried out by actively seeking out new works by writers who are affiliated with the region, and also through national literary competitions which elevate Inlandia Books to the national literary stage.

To learn more about the Inlandia Institute, please visit our website at www.InlandiaInstitute.org.

The Hillary Gravendyk Prize is awarded annually for two full-length collections of poetry: one national and one representing the Inland Southern California region. Each winner receives a monetary prize of $1,000 and book publication through Inlandia Books.

HILLARY GRAVENDYK (1979-2014) was a beloved poet living and teaching in Southern California's "Inland Empire" region. She wrote the acclaimed poetry book *Harm* (Omnidawn, 2012) and the posthumously published *The Soluble Hour* (Omnidawn, 2017) as well as *Unlikely Conditions*, with Cynthia Arrieu-King (1913 Press, 2017) and the poetry chapbook *The Naturalist* (Achiote Press, 2008). A native of Washington State, she was an admired Assistant Professor of English at Pomona College in Claremont, CA. Hillary Gravendyk was two-time winner of the Eisner Prize in Poetry and was awarded a 2015 Pushcart Prize for her poem "Your Ghost," which appeared in the *Pushcart Prize Anthology*. She passed away on May 10, 2014 after a long illness. This contest was established in her memory.

The Hillary Gravendyk Prize Poetry Series

Condition by Meg Reynolds
Winner of the 2024 National Hillary Gravendyk Prize

Surety by Anna Zumbahlen
Winner of the 2024 Regional Hillary Gravendyk Prize

pain survey by Jennifer Mackenzie
Winner of the 2023 National Hillary Gravendyk Prize

Law of the Letter by Elizabeth Galoozis
Winner of the 2023 Regional Hillary Gravendyk Prize

the artemisia by William S. Barnes
Winner of the 2022 National Hillary Gravendyk Prize

Bones Awaiting the Blaze by Tiffany Elliott
Winner of the 2022 Regional Hillary Gravendyk Prize

How to Know You're Dreaming When You're Dreaming by Angelica Maria Barraza Tran
Winner of the 2021 National Hillary Gravendyk Prize

Our Lady of Perpetual Desert by Alexandra Martinez
Winner of the 2021 Regional Hillary Gravendyk Prize

among the enemies by Michael Samra
Winner of the 2020 National Hillary Gravendyk Prize

This Side of the Fire by Jonathan Maule
Winner of the 2020 Regional Hillary Gravendyk Prize

The Silk the Moths Ignore by Bronwen Tate
Winner of the 2019 National Hillary Gravendyk Prize

Remyth: A Postmodernist Ritual by Adam Martinez
Winner of the 2019 Regional Hillary Gravendyk Prize

Former Possessions of the Spanish Empire by Michelle Peñaloza
Winner of the 2018 National Hillary Gravendyk Prize

All the Emergency-Type Structures by Elizabeth Cantwell
Winner of the 2018 Regional Hillary Gravendyk Prize

Our Bruises Kept Singing Purple by Malcolm Friend
Winner of the 2017 National Hillary Gravendyk Prize

Traces of a Fifth Column by Marco Maisto
Winner of the 2016 National Hillary Gravendyk Prize

God's Will for Monsters by Rachelle Cruz
Winner of the 2016 Regional Hillary Gravendyk Prize
Winner of the 2018 American Book Award

Map of an Onion by Kenji C. Liu
Winner of the 2015 National Hillary Gravendyk Prize

All Things Lose Thousands of Times by Angela Peñaredondo
Winner of the 2015 Regional Hillary Gravendyk Prize

www.ingramcontent.com/pod-product-compliance
Lightning Source LLC
LaVergne TN
LVHW011029110826
845149LV00015B/3342
* 9 7 8 1 9 5 5 9 6 9 5 2 9 *